Creative Family
Prayer Times

Creative Family Prayer Times

52 Fun Ways to Pray Together

Mike and Amy Nappa

NAVPRESS

OUR GUARANTEE TO YOU

The Navigators is an international Christian organization. Our mission is to advance the gospel of Jesus and His kingdom into the nations through spiritual generations of laborers living and discipling among the lost. We see a vital movement of the gospel, fueled by prevailing prayer, flowing freely through relational networks and out into the nations where workers for the kingdom are next door to everyone.

© 2007 Nappaland Communications Inc.

www.navpress.com

Content was previously published as *52 Fun Family Prayer Adventures*, copyright © 1996 by Augsburg Fortress.

NAVPRESS, BRINGING TRUTH TO LIFE, *Pray!*, and the NAVPRESS logo are registered trademarks of NavPress. Absence of ® in connection with marks of NavPress or other parties does not indicate an absence of registration of those marks.

This book is published in association with the Nappaland Literary Agency, an independent agency dedicated to publishing works that are: Authentic. Relevant. Eternal. Visit us on the Web at: http://www.Nappaland.com.

ISBN-10: 1600062571
ISBN-13: 9781600062575

Cover Design by J. Bridget Rennie

Visit the *Pray!* magazine Web site at www.praymag.com.

Unless otherwise identified, all Scripture quotations in this publication are taken from the HOLY BIBLE: NEW INTERNATIONAL VERSION® (NIV®). Copyright © 1973, 1978, 1984 by International Bible Society. Used by permission of Zondervan Publishing House. All rights reserved.

Printed in the United States of America

1 2 3 4 5 6 7 8 9 10 / 12 11 10 09 08 07

FOR A FREE CATALOG OF NAVPRESS BOOKS & BIBLE STUDIES,
CALL 1-800-366-7788 (USA) OR 1-800-839-4769 (CANADA).

To our dear friends
Rick and Ellen Frandsen
with whom we've shared many prayers
and many adventures

# Contents

Weekly Prayer Activities

Monthly Prayer Activities

Introduction

We hate to admit but it, but sometimes we get bored by prayer.

Don't get us wrong—prayer *is* one of the most powerful means of communication God has granted us. And it's certainly not God's fault if our minds wander when we're praying. While nothing should be more appealing than spending intimate, personal time with the Lord in prayer, the problem remains that we still can get distracted. And we'll bet that, on occasion, you and your family do, too.

It happens all too often, whether you're praying alone or with others. Your head is bowed and you're ready to pray. Perhaps someone is praying aloud. Then . . .

You think about work. You think about the last song you heard on the radio. You think about the dog barking in the backyard and whether the mail will come early or late. You wonder whether you returned your library book in time to avoid a fine, if you'll be able to get in a few good spikes during the next volleyball game, and on and on. You've forgotten God is listening as you make a mental list of what you must do in the next few hours, days, or weeks.

We know, because we've been there. We find ourselves saying, "Well, we *have* to go pray," instead of "Wow! We *get* to go pray!" And this attitude carries over into our family prayer time. We quickly ramble through our requests as if reading a shopping list. Our time of thanks before a meal is a race to see if the prayer can be finished before someone starts to eat anyway.

But instead of assuming that boredom during prayer must be endured, we decided to do something about it. The results were this book—and an answer to prayer.

In *Creative Family Prayer Times*, you'll find a collection of innovative ideas to help you focus your family devotions and add meaning to the words you say. These ideas aren't meant to replace what you already do during family prayer time, but instead are designed to bring a change of pace in a hands-on, involving way to your existing prayer life.

Since we can talk to God anytime and anyplace, we've included a wide variety of prayer activities. Some are to be shared at dinner or just before bedtime; others are to be experienced on a Saturday morning or during a family outing. Some activities can be done alone, while others include everyone.

As you read through the ideas in this book, you'll notice some involve daily participation and others involve projects that last for a week, a month, or even a year. Remember, you don't have to use these ideas all at once. Pick and choose the ones that will work best for your family, or modify others to your liking.

We want prayer to be an exciting part of our everyday lives, and we hope this book will help do the same for your family life.

DAILY

Prayer Activities

Breaking Through

Focus: Obstacles to prayer

For this prayer activity you'll need a sheet of blank newsprint or wrapping paper that will cover a doorway in your home. You'll also need a marker and tape.

Gather your family for a time of prayer. Read James 5:13–16 aloud, and discuss why God wants us to talk to Him. Then ask, "What things keep you from praying?"

As family members give their answers, write them on the large sheet of paper. Share your own reasons as well. Then ask family members what obstacles there are to your family taking time to pray together; write them down too.

When everyone has responded and all answers are written, tape the sheet of paper over an open doorway. Then ask your family members to join with you in breaking through these barriers to prayer. (Let younger children break through the paper first.) When everyone has gone through the doorway, gather on the other side for a time of prayer. Pray that God will help your family overcome these obstacles so that individually and together you can grow closer to God by communicating with Him.

You may also want to take this time to plan a regular time to pray as a group. Many families pray together at meals, in the morning, or at bedtime. If you already pray at these times, we encourage you to continue. But you may also want to set aside a short period of time one day a week, such as fifteen minutes every Sunday night or following dinner on Mondays, when everyone can come together to share and pray.

~ • ~

> *What other nation is so great as to have their gods near them the way the LORD our God is near us whenever we pray to him?*
>
> DEUTERONOMY 4:7

ABCs of Adoration Book

Focus: Adoration of God

Get twenty-six sheets of paper and write one letter of the alphabet on the top of each one. Starting with the page labeled "A," have your family work together to list all of the things they admire about God that begin with that letter.

For example, on the "A" page, you might list

- awesome power,
- affectionate love, and
- activity in my life.

The "B" page might include

- beautiful creation,
- blessings, and
- the Bible that tells me about God.

Once your family has thought of at least one thing to write on each page (good luck with "Q" and "X"!), put the pages in a notebook or simply staple them together. Then use this book as a guide for family prayers.

Open to one of the alphabet pages, and begin your family's prayer by saying, "Lord, You are worthy to be adored. We know because of these things . . ." and read to God the list for that letter. Let family members take turns choosing a page from your book to pray through. As you and your family pray, explain why the items you listed are qualities you admire about God.

Keep this book in a convenient place. Encourage everyone to add new attributes as they think of them.

⌢ • ⌢

David praised the LORD in the presence of the whole assembly, saying, "Praise be to you, O LORD, God of our father Israel, from everlasting to everlasting."

I CHRONICLES 29:10

Coins in a Fountain

Focus: Forgiveness

Collect a handful of coins (pennies, nickels, dimes, or quarters), and place them in a small cup or similar container. Take this cup and go with your family to a fountain for a time of prayer. (Check the local mall, library, or a city building to find a fountain, but make sure the fountain doesn't have fish in it.)

As you stand or sit together in front of the fountain, pass the container of coins and have each person select one. Explain to them that this is a time for each person to tell God that he or she is sorry for any sins committed that week.

Each person should pray, "Lord, in this past week I know I've disappointed you in this way . . ." and finish by confessing to God one way he or she has fallen short spiritually. Then, toss the coin into the water. If anyone is too embarrassed to share a confession aloud, allow him or her to pray silently before tossing a coin.

Repeat this confessing and coin-tossing process as many times as you like. When everyone is done, ask family members to dip their hands in the fountain's water for a quick washing.

Then close your family prayer with "Thank you, God, for the promise of Your forgiveness that buries our sins as this fountain has 'buried' our coins, and that washes our hearts as this water has washed our hands. In Jesus' name, amen."

~ • ~

But I pray to you, O LORD, in the time of your favor; in your great love, O God, answer me with your sure salvation.

PSALM 69:13

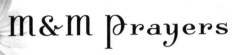

M&M Prayers

Focus: Praying for others

Pass around a bag or bowl of M&Ms the next time your family is gathered for prayer. Let each person take a handful, but don't let anyone eat the candies yet. Explain that the color of the candies will indicate the direction of the family's prayers. Lead them in prayer using this guide and stopping for prayer after explaining each color. Say:

- "For every green M&M you chose, pray for your spouse (present or future) or some other significant person in your life." This is a great way to get kids thinking about what qualities they want to find in a future mate. Encourage them to pray for this person's safety, spiritual and physical growth, and so on.
- "For every red M&M you chose, pray for a member of your family by name (a parent, son, daughter, brother, sister, grandchild, niece, nephew)."
- "For every orange M&M you chose, pray for a teacher in your life (a coworker, a professor, a pastor, a Bible study leader, a school teacher, a mentor)."
- "For every yellow M&M you chose, pray for one of your neighbors (near your home, an office mate, a person whose desk is near yours at school)."

- "For every dark brown M&M you chose, pray for a leader in your life (a politician, a local businessperson, a celebrity, a member of your church's staff, the president)."
- "For every light brown M&M you chose, pray for Christians in other countries."

This might be best used as an *after*-dinner prayer time. Repeat this process as often as your family's calorie intake allows.

⁓ • ⁓

Then you will call upon me and come and pray to me, and I will listen to you.

JEREMIAH 29:12

Playground Prayers

Focus: Praying for children

Visit a nearby playground or park where children play. If your kids want, allow them to join in the activities of the playground. Then sit in an inconspicuous spot and simply watch the kids as they run and tumble, laugh and cry.

When you're ready, begin praying for a specific child on the playground. Use what you see in that child as a tool to focus your prayer.

For example, if you notice a boy is particularly adventuresome and prone to take risks, pray that God would channel that bold spirit into ways that would lead him to discover more about God. (You might also pray for that child's safety and protection.)

Or, if you observe a girl who plays alone and seems disconnected from the other kids, you might pray that God would surround her with people who can become deep, meaningful friends.

If you spot a child who is unkind, you could pray that God will change his or her heart to be one that seeks God and takes an interest in others.

If your children are playing as well, pray specifically for each one. If they are sitting with you, have them join you in prayer for those playing, being sure they have a chance to talk to God about the children they see.

As you pray, ask God to direct your prayers for each child. Finish with a prayer for all the children you see to experience God's love in a tangible way throughout the rest of their lives. Pray for as many children as time allows.

～ • ～

And this is my prayer: that your love may abound more and more in knowledge and depth of insight.

PHILIPPIANS 1:9

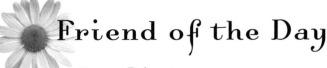

Friend of the Day

Focus: Friends

Each night as you pray with your child before bed, let him or her choose a friend to include in your prayers. Some children will enjoy selecting friends randomly, while others may want to create a list or even post a bulletin board with pictures of friends to use as a reference. Allow your child to decide who to pray for—even if he or she chooses the same friend for several nights in a row.

If your little one would like to, have him or her pray aloud for the chosen friend. Or, take turns praying. Here are a few ideas of how to pray:

- Pray for the child's spiritual growth. "Help [fill in name] to know You love him, Lord. Thank You that he learns about You at church." Or, "Help me show [fill in name] that You love her, Father. Even though her family doesn't know about You, I pray that she learns about You from me and from other people who know You."
- Pray for specific needs as you are aware of them. "Jesus, watch over [fill in name] as she takes a test tomorrow." Or, "Help my friend get over his cold, Father."

- Pray for the relationship between this child and your child. "Thank you, Lord, for giving my son friends. Help [fill in name] be an example of Your love."
- You may occasionally ask your child to pray for a child he or she doesn't consider to be a friend. "God, show Your love to [fill in name]. May the relationship between us improve over time."

~ • ~

We always thank God, the Father of our Lord Jesus Christ, when we pray for you.

COLOSSIANS 1:3

Prayer Toss

Focus: Prayer for family members

For this idea, you'll need a sheet of paper and a pencil for each person. Have each family member write his or her name and a prayer request on his or her paper. (Ask older children to help younger ones who can't yet read.) The prayer requests can be for anything this family member feels is important.

When everyone is ready, stand in a circle and instruct them to crumple up their papers and toss them in the air so they fall into the center of the circle. Wait to see where each paper wad lands. Then have family members pick up the paper nearest to where they are standing. Say, "Pray for the person whose paper you picked up."

If you like, spend time with each person silently praying over the request they have read, then recrumple the papers and repeat the activity and time of prayer. Let everyone know it's okay to pray for the same person twice, or even to pray for his or her own request.

After doing this several times, have each person save the paper picked up last and use it as a reminder to pray for that family member over the next week.

Devote yourselves to prayer, being watchful and thankful.

COLOSSIANS 4:2

Sunrise Watch

Focus: A quiet time of thanks

This prayer activity may be the most difficult one in this entire book—it requires getting up before the sun rises! If you can entice your whole family out of bed (do you smell bacon sizzling?) before the crack of dawn, include everyone in this time of prayer. Or, you may want to use it on a special occasion when two family members are up early for a fishing expedition or when a parent is still up after soothing a sick child through the night. If all else fails, you could use this idea during a sunset instead.

Here's what to do: Find a place where you can see the sunrise clearly. If the view from your windows isn't good, go to a park or a scenic overlook. Then settle down to watch the first rays of dawn peak through the dark.

Each time you see a new color in the sky, thank God for something beautiful. For example, as pink glows in the sky, thank God for the smile of a friend. As the sky turns orange, thank God for the sweet friendship of family members. As yellow shines through, thank God for the beauty of a favorite flower. Continue in your time of thanks until the sun is shining brightly.

Then head to breakfast with a smile of thanksgiving on your face.

Note: Because looking directly into the sun can damage vision, be sure to caution children to look at the sky around the sun, not directly at the sun itself.

⁓ • ⁓

We ought always to thank God for you, brothers, and rightly so, because your faith is growing more and more, and the love every one of you has for each other is increasing.

2 THESSALONIANS 1:3

Pantomime Prayer

Focus: Communicating through actions

When your family gathers to pray, have each person think of one prayer or praise he or she would like to express to God. Then say, "Think of a way to pantomime, or act out without using words, your thoughts to God. For example, if you want to apologize to God for doing the wrong thing, you might kneel and cover your face with your hands. If you want to thank God for His work in your life, you might stand and applaud."

Give everyone a moment of "think time." Then your family can proceed in one of these ways:

1. Everyone can pantomime his or her thoughts to God at the same time. In this way, each person is concerned only with his or her own prayer.
2. One family member can begin by sharing his or her prayer and how it can be expressed. Then the entire family can pantomime that person's prayer, corporately praying without words.

Close your time of prayer by offering thanks together using this physical expression.

Is any one of you in trouble? He should pray. Is anyone happy? Let him sing songs of praise.

JAMES 5:13

Seed Spittin' Prayer

Focus: Outdoor prayer time

U se this prayer adventure during the hot summer months when everyone wants to be outside. You'll need a watermelon, a knife, and sidewalk chalk.

Draw a large tic-tac-toe board on your driveway or other cement surface. In four of the nine squares write the following words: *Thanks*, *Praise*, *Forgive*, and *Help*. Then explain to your family members the meaning of each word.

- *Thanks* is simply thanking God for something He has done.
- *Praise* is telling God something good about Himself, such as "God, You are powerful!"
- *Forgive* means to ask God to forgive you for something you've done wrong.
- *Help* is to ask God for help in some area of your life.

Have your family choose other words to fill in the remaining five squares. You may want to write the names of family members, friends, teachers, or church staff. Or, you may choose words like *vacation*, *sunshine*, or *the Bible*.

When each square has a word written in it, cut the watermelon and give each person a large slice. Have everyone stand or sit near the chalked tic-tac-toe board.

Say, "Spit your seeds onto this tic-tac-toe board. Wherever your seed lands, pray as the words direct. For example, if your seed lands on *Praise*, tell God something great about Himself. If it lands on a person's name, thank God for that person or pray for God to help that person."

Let this be a fun time of spitting seeds and praying one-sentence prayers aloud. Keep the prayers and seeds going as long as the watermelon lasts! Then get out the hose and wash the seeds and chalk away.

⌒ ● ⌒

I urge, then, first of all, that requests, prayers, intercession and thanksgiving be made for everyone.

I TIMOTHY 2:1

Real Estate Prayer

Focus: Prayer for our home

This prayer activity will take your family on a walking tour of the place you live. As you meet for prayer, explain that you'll be moving through each room of your house or apartment and praying for the people and activities represented by that room.

Begin in your living room. Pray for the time the family spends together in this room. Ask God to guide conversations that take place here and to let those who visit in this room know His love. Let any family member pray who wants to pray, then move to the next room.

When you arrive at the bedrooms, pray for those who sleep there. Pray in specific ways for each person and for God's blessing upon those who come into this room each day.

In the kitchen pray for family times together at meals. Ask that these be a time of laughter and harmony. Thank God for the gift of food.

Continue through your home, including areas such as the front entry and hallways. You might even want to include your yard, garage, parking place, or apartment swimming pool. Thank God for His provision of a home, and ask that it would be a place where people experience God's love.

Close your time together by reading Joshua 24:15: "As for me and my household, we will serve the LORD." Ask God to help everyone in your household serve Him no matter what room he or she is in!

━◦ • ◦━

Do not be anxious about anything, but in everything, by prayer and petition, with thanksgiving, present your requests to God.

PHILIPPIANS 4:6

I Remember

Focus: People and memories from the past

Pull out old photo albums, and take a trip down memory lane.
Gather everyone on the couch or a bed, and reminisce about vacations, holidays, school events, and other occasions. Take your time looking through the pictures, and allow different family members to tell their memories of when each picture was taken.

Soon you'll be hearing things like, "That was the Christmas Mom had the flu and we got to order pizza!" and "Remember when Mr. Cunningham lived next door and we used to eat the strawberries from his garden?"

As you remember these fun times, stop occasionally to pray. When pictures remind you of a fun vacation, thank God for the time you were able to have fun and see new places. If a snapshot brings back memories of someone who has since died, ask God to continue to heal old wounds. Thank Him for the lives and memories you have of these loved ones.

When you come upon pictures of long-lost friends, pray that God will continue to show Himself to these friends. You may even want to find a person you'd forgotten about to ask forgiveness for a past wrong or to share with this friend about God's love. Or, if friends pictured are still an active part of your lives, ask God to build your friendships and thank Him for putting these people in your lives.

You may have pictures of family members who no longer live with you, such as a daughter who has gone away to college or a father who isn't at home anymore because of divorce or military deployment. Remember to thank God for these people and to bring their needs before Him as well.

 ~ • ~

Enter his gates with thanksgiving and his courts with praise; give thanks to him and praise his name.

PSALM 100:4

Wet-Head Prayers

Focus: Praying for family members

F ill several small balloons with water, and place them in a bucket or similar container. Have your family meet outside in your yard or at a local park.

Everyone needs to stand in a circle. (If only two people are participating, they should face each other.) Give each person a water balloon. Explain that on the count of three, everyone should throw his or her balloon into the air and try to catch a *different* balloon. Then count to three and let the balloons soar and the water splash! Continue tossing the balloons into the air until a balloon is broken.

As soon as one balloon breaks, stop tossing and together determine who got the wettest. Then have another family member pray for this person. The prayer can be short, but it should focus on thanking God for him or her and naming qualities others find special or on specific requests this family member has shared.

Then arm everyone again with balloons, and begin tossing them again. Each time one or more balloons break, repeat the process. It's okay to pray for the same person more than once. Also, encourage different family members to pray each time.

You may find it "necessary" to bomb a family member who

continues to remain dry. Remember, *everyone* needs prayer!

When everyone is thoroughly soaked, pass out the towels. The next time it's sunny, see if anyone wants to be refreshed again with a cooling prayer!

$$\sim \bullet \sim$$

They devoted themselves to the apostles' teaching and to the fellowship, to the breaking of bread and to prayer.

ACTS 2:42

Anywhere Prayer

Focus: God hears us everywhere

With your young children, read Psalm 139:1–4. Explain the meaning of this passage: God knows everything about us, including our thoughts. Then read verses 7–12, which say there is no place we can go where God is not there.

As you discuss this with your family, ask, "Can you think of any place we could go where God would not be there and would not hear our prayers?"

Take your family into a closet or another cramped, dark space. Ask, "Do you think God can hear us here?" Assure them that the Bible says God will hear us anywhere, then pray right there, thanking God for hearing you.

Then ask your kids to think of another place to go. This might be in the car, the basement, the backyard shed, or under a bed. Go to as many places as your children want, squish in together, and pray!

This adventure is especially reassuring to young children who may be afraid of being alone in the dark. God can always hear them, and they can talk to Him wherever they are!

I will tell of the kindnesses of the LORD, the deeds for which he is to be praised, according to all the LORD has done for us—yes, the many good things he has done for the house of Israel, according to his compassion and many kindnesses.

ISAIAH 63:7

Bouquet of Blessings

Focus: Flowers as symbols of prayer

Traditionally, different plants and flowers symbolize a variety of emotions and messages. The following is a list of meanings that have been given to some popular flowers.

- rose — love
- white chrysanthemum — truth
- white daisy — innocence
- gladiolus — strength of character
- iris — message
- ivy — friendship
- lily of the valley — happiness
- marigold — grief
- violet — faithfulness
- zinnia — thoughts of absent friends

Visit your local florist and collect a variety of these flowers. Then when you later join your family for a time of prayer, give each person one or more of the flowers. Share the flowers' meanings, then ask each person to pray according to their flower's meaning. For example,

- a person with an iris could thank God for the message of love He sent through Jesus, or God's message that we read in the Bible.
- if someone has a marigold, he or she could pray for those who are experiencing grief because of sickness, loss of a loved one, or other difficult times.
- the holder of a rose could thank God for His love or for the love of family members, or ask God to help family members to show love to each other and those outside the family.

Let family members think of different ways to use the symbolism of their flower to express thoughts of thanks, praise, and need to God. When your prayer time is over, gather the flowers into a bouquet as a reminder of the prayers you have offered, or give the bouquet to someone for whom you have prayed.

~ • ~

And when you stand praying, if you hold anything against anyone, forgive him, so that your Father in heaven may forgive you your sins.

MARK 11:25

In Motion

Focus: The Lord's Prayer

Read Luke 11:1–4 with your family. Talk about what the words and phrases of this prayer mean. Then have your family work together to create motions that express the meaning of the prayer.

For example, your family might express the word *hallowed* by making motions like the washing of hands, as this word means "holy or pure." At "lead us not into temptation" you might hold your hands beside your eyes as if they were blinders. The younger your children are, the more concrete or realistic your actions will need to be. Older children may enjoy creating more abstract actions to express the words and phrases.

When you've created actions to express the entire prayer, say the prayer aloud together, making the appropriate motions. As you practice this prayer, you'll soon be able to use only the motions to express the thoughts in the prayer.

⌒ • ⌒

One day Jesus was praying in a certain place. When he finished, one of his disciples said to him, "Lord, teach us to pray, just as John taught his disciples."

LUKE 11:1

Porch Listen

Focus: Praying for the world around us

Go outside and sit together on your porch, patio, or in your back-yard. If you don't have an area such as these, go to a local park, spread a blanket, and sit together.

Tell your family to listen quietly to the sounds around. After three to five minutes of silence, say, "Now let's talk to God about the different sounds we hear." Then begin with short, sentence prayers as you are guided by the noises around you. For example,

- pray for the neighbor children whose voices you hear.
- thank God for all creation as you listen to crickets chirping.
- as you hear birds singing, thank God for music.
- if you hear the siren of a fire engine, pray for the safety of those who are waiting for help.

Finish by thanking God for each family member.

During the days of Jesus' life on earth, he offered up prayers and petitions with loud cries and tears to the one who could save him from death, and he was heard because of his reverent submission.

HEBREWS 5:7

Fishing for Compliments

Focus: Praising God

For this activity, you'll need to make a fishing pole. Tie two or three feet of string to a stick, tree branch, or a yardstick. At the end of the string tie a hook made from a paper clip. Next, take the cardboard roll from an empty roll of toilet paper or paper towels. Cut this into five to ten circles. (It's okay if they get a little bent in the cutting process.)

Ask your family to think of things they'd like to compliment God on, such as the great job He did making flowers, the gift of His love, His incredible power, and so on. As family members think of praises for God, write each compliment on the outside of a different cardboard circle.

When you've used all the circles, place them in a pile on the floor. Pass the fishing pole around and let each person "fish" for a cardboard ring. (For younger children, be sure the rolls are standing on their sides for easier hooking. Also, shorten the string by rolling it around the stick a few times.)

When each person has fished for and "caught" a compliment, take turns praising God. Then continue fishing and praising until all the cardboard rolls have been caught.

Praise be to the God and Father of our Lord Jesus Christ, the Father of compassion and the God of all comfort.

2 CORINTHIANS 1:3

Songs of Prayer

Focus: Communicating through music

Have each family member choose a hymn or praise song that expresses a theme about which he or she would like to pray. For example, if someone is thankful that Jesus is his or her best friend, that person might pick "What a Friend We Have in Jesus." A grandmother who is thankful for the love expressed through her own family or the church family could select "Blest Be the Tie That Binds." A family member wanting to praise God's glory might choose "Oh, for a Thousand Tongues to Sing." Even the youngest family members can participate with songs like "Jesus Loves Me" and "Awesome God."

It may be helpful to have a couple of hymnals or songbooks on hand to use as reference. Or, let younger kids look through their music collections to find songs that express their thoughts. Some family members might enjoy the challenge of writing an original song or new words to a familiar tune.

When everyone has chosen a song, start with the youngest person and take turns sharing what your song is and why you've selected it. Tell how this song expresses your thoughts, thanks, or praises to or about God.

Then sing each song as a prayer to God. If any family members play musical instruments, have them accompany you. Or, sing along with a tape or CD. You could also sing your prayers a cappella.

But you are a chosen people, a royal priesthood, a holy nation, a people belonging to God, that you may declare the praises of him who called you out of darkness into his wonderful light.

I PETER 2:9

Make a Joyful Noise

Focus: Laughter

For this activity, you'll need a tape recorder. Before your family prayer time, tape each family member laughing for ten to fifteen seconds. This may test your joke-telling or tickling abilities! Leave a break of about five seconds between each person on tape. Don't forget to include yourself.

Have everyone sit around the tape recorder. Begin the time of prayer by completing this prayer: "Lord, something you brought into my life that brings laughter and smiles is . . ." Then play the laughter of the first person you taped. When you come to the break, turn off the tape. Hearing the tape is sure to bring more laughter as family members recognize their own voices or guess who is laughing.

Have the next person in the circle complete the same sentence prayer, thanking God for someone or something that has brought laughter and smiles to his or her life. After this person has prayed, play the voice of another family member laughing. Repeat this until each family member has prayed, and each laughing voice has been heard. When you've said "Amen," tape yourselves laughing as a family. Let your voices of merriment be a joyful sound to God!

> *From the rising of the sun to the place where it sets, the name of the LORD is to be praised.*

PSALM 113:3

Birds of Pray

Focus: We are important to God

You'll need a birdfeeder for this activity. If your family already owns one, fill it with bird seed. If not, consider purchasing a kit and assembling the feeder together as a family project. Or, try one of these simple and easy-to-make feeders:

- Cut a hole in the side of an empty two-liter soft-drink bottle to serve as a "door" for the birds. Fill the bottle up to this hole with bird seed. The bottle can be hung from the top with a string or set on the ground in a patio or balcony area.
- Spread peanut butter into the crevices of a large pinecone. Roll the pinecone in birdseed until the peanut butter is covered. Hang this from a tree or an awning.

Whatever birdfeeder you choose, place it in a location where you'll be able to see the birds without disturbing them. Then read this verse together.

> *Look at the birds of the air; they do not sow or reap or store away in barns, and yet your heavenly Father feeds them.*

Are you not much more valuable than they?

MATTHEW 6:26

Ask family members to describe how they know they're important to God (God sent Jesus, God forgives us, God provides for our needs, the Bible says so, etc.).

Then say, "Every time we see a bird at our feeder, let's stop to thank God that we're important to Him."

Fill your birdfeeder often, and as you enjoy the beauty of the colorful flying creatures God has created, take time to thank Him for creating and loving you!

⁓ • ⁓

With my mouth I will greatly extol the LORD; in the great throng I will praise him.

PSALM 109:30

Heavenly Hallelujahs

Focus: The "Hallelujah" chorus

For this adventure you'll need a recording of the "Hallelujah" chorus from Handel's *Messiah*. You should be able to check out a copy of one at your local library.

Gather your family and read aloud the following story.

> *In 1741 a man named Charles Jennens compiled different verses from the Bible that told the story of Jesus. He gave this collection to George F. Handel, a composer. Handel took only twenty-four days to write the music that accompanied these words. This was called* Messiah. *When Handel had written the part that is called the "Hallelujah" chorus, his servant found him with tears in his eyes. Handel had found such beauty in the words and music he told his servant, "I think I did see all heaven before me, and the great God Himself!"*
>
> *When* Messiah *was performed a few years later, the king of England attended a performance. He was so moved by the "Hallelujah" chorus that he stood up and remained standing for the entire song. It was the custom that everyone stand when the king stands, so the entire audience stood for the remainder as well. This tradition has continued, and now it is customary to stand whenever you hear the "Hallelujah" chorus.*

Have a family member read Revelation 11:15 and 19:6–7. Explain that the words of these verses are used in the "Hallelujah" chorus. Then discuss these questions with your family.

- What do these verses make you think about heaven?
- What do you think it will be like when we're all in heaven and singing praises to God?

Next, listen to the "Hallelujah" chorus. Play it as loudly as you can! (You may stand if you like!) When the music is over, ask,

- How do you think these voices singing praise are like the voices of people in heaven singing to God?
- How does this music make you feel?
- How do you think God feels when He hears us singing praises to Him like this?

Play the music again, and this time encourage family members to sing along, praising God like the angels!

~ • ~

But when you pray, go into your room, close the door and pray to your Father, who is unseen. Then your Father, who sees what is done in secret, will reward you.

MATTHEW 6:6

Sin Slam-Dunk

Focus: Forgiveness from each other and from God

Provide blank paper and pens or pencils for your family. Have each person take a sheet of paper, and write one or more sins he or she has committed that they'd like to ask God forgiveness for. Younger family members can draw a picture or have someone help them with the writing. Allow enough time for everyone to write as many things as he or she wants.

If you like, give family members the option of sharing what they've written, but it's not necessary. Next, place a wastebasket in the center of the room. Stand in a circle around the basket, and have each person crumple his or her paper into a ball. Then pray together, asking God for forgiveness for the things written on the paper.

Take turns "slam-dunking" your paper balls into the trash. When all the paper has made its way into the basket, join hands and thank Jesus for "slam-dunking" the penalty of sin.

Pray also for me, that whenever I open my mouth, words may be given me so that I will fearlessly make known the mystery of the gospel.

EPHESIANS 6:19

Outside-in Prayer

Focus: Family

Meet as a family in the largest room of your house or apartment, and stand against the walls as far from each other as possible. Explain that after each prayer request is prayed for, everyone should take a large step toward the center of the room.

Here are some suggestions of what to pray about:

- Praise God for creating families.
- Pray for God to forgive family members when they don't treat each other well.
- Ask Him to help those in the family to act kindly toward each other.
- Thank God for sending Jesus to help us all know how to behave.
- Ask God to help family members be examples of Jesus' love to each other every day.

As soon as everyone in your family has reached the middle of the room, join together in a family group hug, and close your time by thanking God for each person that makes up your special family.

If you believe, you will receive whatever you ask for in prayer.

MATTHEW 21:22

Musical Prayers

Focus: Praying for family members

This activity is similar to "Musical Chairs," but everyone wins! You'll need five pieces of paper in these colors: red, orange, blue, green, and brown. (If you don't have one or more of these colors, substitute another color and adjust the directions as necessary.) The papers should be at least the size of a playing card. If you have more than five people in your family, use two papers of each color. You will also need a radio or tape or CD player and one person appointed to turn the music on and off.

Place the pieces of paper in a large circle on the floor. You may want to tape them down to be sure they stay where they are put! Have each family member (including you) stand on a piece of paper. Then start the music. While the music is playing, have family members walk around the circle counterclockwise from paper to paper. When you stop the music, have each person stop on the paper closest to him or her. Then take turns praying as follows:

- If you are standing on a red paper, pray for the adults in your family. This can include grandparents, aunts, uncles, as well as moms and dads.

- If you are standing on an orange paper, pray for the person behind you.
- If you are standing on a blue paper, pray for each child in your family. If you want, include cousins or family members not living with you (such as stepsiblings or older children).
- If you're standing on a green paper, pray for the person in front of you.
- If you're standing on a brown paper, pray for yourself!

After each person has prayed, start the music again and get moving! When you stop the music, family members should be on different colors and can pray again according to their new color. Repeat the music and praying sequence as many times as you and your family want.

I will give thanks to the LORD because of his righteousness and will sing praise to the name of the LORD Most High.

PSALM 7:17

Prayer for Heroes

Focus: People we admire

Before you meet for prayer, ask each family member to choose one living person whom they admire or consider to be a hero or heroine. This person could be an athlete, a singer, an actor, a politician, a scientist, and so on. If possible, have family members find an item that represents this person such as a picture, a CD, a copy of his or her latest book; and bring it to prayer time.

When you've gathered together, take turns telling about the person you admire. Share why this person is important to you and what you like about him or her. After everyone has shared, take time to pray for each hero. If you know the person is a Christian, pray that he or she will grow stronger spiritually and will continue to follow God. If this person isn't a Christian or you aren't sure, pray that this hero will learn of God's love and accept His forgiveness. Remember to ask God to bless their families, careers, and the impact they have on those around them.

After you've prayed, take time to write to each person for whom you've prayed. In brief notes, express your admiration, and let this person know you're praying for him or her. If you'd like to hear back from this person, include your name and address (a self-addressed, stamped envelope is always helpful too!).

If you don't know the address to send your letters to, check the library or Internet. But even if you can't locate an address, keep praying for these people. God knows where they are!

And when you pray, do not be like the hypocrites, for they love to pray standing in the synagogues and on the street corners to be seen by men. I tell you the truth, they have received their reward in full.

MATTHEW 6:5

Gone with the Wind

Focus: Saying you're sorry

For this prayer time, you'll need several blown-up balloons. You may use helium balloons if you like, but ones that you inflate yourself will work just as well.

Give each family member a balloon and a pen (permanent markers work best). Ask them to think of something they've done wrong that they'd like God to forget about, and have them write one or two words on the balloon to represent what they've done. For example, if Emma is sorry she called Jared a mean name, she might write "mean name" on her balloon. If Kadeem is sorry he took Dad's car without asking, he could write, "car." Have older family members help those who cannot write yet.

When everyone is ready, have different family members volunteer to read aloud the following verses.

> *As far as the east is from the west, so far has he removed our transgressions from us.*
>
> PSALM 103:12

*If we confess our sins, he is faithful and just and will forgive
us our sins and purify us from all unrighteousness.*

1 JOHN 1:9

Be sure all family members know the meanings of words such as
transgressions, confess, just, purify, and *unrighteousness.* Discuss together
what these verses mean.

Then begin a time of prayer, asking God for forgiveness for what
is written on your balloon. After you've prayed, pop your balloon with
a thumbtack or pin to represent God forgiving and forgetting about
your sin. Then pass the pin to another family member and allow him
or her to pray then pop his or her balloon. Continue until all balloons
have been popped. Ask family members how popping a balloon is like
sins being gone. Close by thanking God for being true to His word and
forgiving our sins.

⁓ • ⁓

*These I will bring to my holy mountain and give them joy in
my house of prayer. Their burnt offerings and sacrifices will
be accepted on my altar; for my house will be called a house of
prayer for all nations.*

ISAIAH 56:7

Stations of Prayer

Focus: Different kinds of prayer

Before your family gathers for a time of prayer, determine four separate areas of a room or of your home that can be used for prayer. This could be the four corners of a room or four separate rooms. These will be four prayer "stations."

Take four pieces of paper, and at the top of each write one of the following words: *Praise*, *Thanks*, *Request*, and *Confession*. Then put one of the papers at each of the four stations.

When your family meets to pray, explain that you'll be taking time individually to pray at the different prayer stations. Show everyone where the stations are located, and give the following instructions:

- At the Praise station, tell God why you think He's wonderful. Say a prayer or sing a song of praise.
- At the Thanks station, thank God for what He's done.
- At the Request station, tell God your needs and the needs of others.
- At the Confession station, tell God you're sorry for things you've done wrong and ask Him to forgive you.

Have each family member go to a different station. (If your family has more than four members, two people can be at the same station at the same time, but ask them to pray individually.) Explain that everyone will stay at his or her station and pray as directed for two to three minutes. (You can make this time shorter if you have younger children or longer if you have older children.)

Begin your prayer time. After two minutes (or whatever amount of time you have decided upon) has passed, have everyone switch stations. Repeat the process until each person has had a chance to pray at each station.

Note: If one or more of your children is under age four, this activity can be done with the entire family together at each station, or an adult can visit each station with the child to guide him or her in prayer.

⁓ • ⁓

> *The* LORD *detests the sacrifice of the wicked, but the prayer of the upright pleases him.*
>
> PROVERBS 15:8

Finger Prayer

Focus: A child's prayer

Small children will love this finger play that guides them through a time of prayer. Use it with your whole family, letting the younger children lead!

Have everyone say aloud,

- My thumb is smallest it's plain to see. It's a reminder to pray for me!
- My pointing finger shows me where to go. I'll pray for those who guide me as I grow.
- My middle finger stands so tall, I'll thank God because He watches over all.
- Finger number four is weaker than the rest. Please God, care for those who need Your rest.
- My very last finger is tiny like a child. I'll pray for other kids across the whole world wide.

As your family recites each line together and refers to the indicated finger, stop for a moment to pray as directed by the rhyme.

Mike & Amy Nappa

—   •   —

May my prayer be set before you like incense; may the lifting up of my hands be like the evening sacrifice.

PSALM 141:2

Instrument of Prayer

Focus: Peace

R ead the following prayer, which is commonly attributed to
St. Francis of Assisi, aloud to your family:

> *Lord, make me an instrument of your peace*
> *Where there is hatred, let me sow love,*
> *Where there is injury, pardon,*
> *Where there is doubt, faith,*
> *Where there is despair, hope,*
> *Where there is darkness, light,*
> *Where there is sadness, joy.*
> *O Divine Master, grant that I may not so much seek to be*
> *   consoled as to console,*
> *not so much to be understood as to understand,*
> *not so much to be loved, as to love;*
> *for it is in giving that we receive,*
> *it is in pardoning that we are pardoned,*
> *it is in dying, that we awake to eternal life.*

After reading the prayer, discuss what it means to different family
members. Then discuss the following:

- The person praying this prayer asks God to make him or her an instrument of God's peace. What kind of "instrument" do you think the writer means?
- How can you be an instrument of peace?

Have each person think of a tool or instrument that could be used to symbolize peace. For example, a hammer could be an instrument of peace if it represents building up others. A wind chime could mean sounds of harmony. A rope might bind people together in unity.

If possible, have family members actually go and get the item they are thinking of. Then let each person explain how his or her instrument symbolizes peace.

Take turns praying. Ask each person to pray that God would make him or her an instrument like the one they have chosen. For example, "Lord, help me to be like these ear plugs. They make things quiet, and I want to be quiet when I think about You." When everyone has prayed, again read the prayer of St. Francis aloud as your closing prayer and request.

$$\sim \; \bullet \; \sim$$

We are glad whenever we are weak but you are strong; and our prayer is for your perfection.

2 CORINTHIANS 13:9

WEEKLY

Prayer Activities

Thanks for the Memories

Focus: Thanking God for responding to prayers

Start a memory box in which you will collect mementos to remind you and your family of God's active presence in your lives.

Begin by having family members decorate a shoebox. You can use wrapping paper, construction paper, stickers, glitter, markers— whatever you like. Then tell your family, "Each time we notice God working in response to one of our prayers, we'll find something that will remind us of what God has done and put it in this box."

Give examples, such as,

- if a friend recovers from an illness, you might put a get-well card in the box,
- if God provides for you financially, you could add a check stub,
- if you pray for guidance and God leads you in a certain direction, you may want to add a compass or road map,
- if you pray for help on a test and do well, consider putting in a page of your class notes into the box.

After a week of collecting items in your memory box, look through it as a family. Use it to remind everyone of reasons for thanking God. Include in your prayers that week a time of thanksgiving when you open the box and take out the mementos one by one. As you examine each item, have the family member who chose it thank God for what it represents and for the way He has worked in the past week.

At this point the box can be emptied and your family can start over, or you may wish to leave these mementos in the box to serve as long-term reminders of God's work. Continue to add to the box as often as you like, using it whenever you need a reminder of how God has answered your family's prayers.

I praise you because I am fearfully and wonderfully made; your works are wonderful, I know that full well.

PSALM 139:14

God's Instructions

Focus: Praying as the Bible directs

This prayer adventure is great for families with kids in junior or senior high. During the next week, read a different passage each day from the following list. Discuss the questions, then let your prayers be led by what you've learned.

DAY ONE: Ps. 122 — THE PEACE OF JERUSALEM
- What is the significance of Jerusalem in this passage?
- Why does the psalmist command the reader to "pray for the peace of Jerusalem"?
- What meaning does this command mean for us today?

DAY TWO: MATT. 5:43–48 AND LUKE 6:27–36 — PERSECUTORS
- What prayer is commanded in these passages?
- Why is it important to pray for our enemies?
- How can you bless an enemy?

DAY THREE: MARK 13:32–37 — WATCH AND PRAY
- What is this passage discussing?
- Why is it necessary to be alert and praying?
- According to this passage, how should you be acting and praying?

Day Four: 2 Thess. 3:1–2 and Heb. 13:18 — Prayer for missionaries

- Who is requesting prayer in these passages, and why?
- Who do you know in similar positions to the writers of these passages?
- How can your prayers help these people?

Day Five: Matt. 9:36–38 — Harvest

- What kind of harvest is Jesus referring to?
- Who are the workers Jesus wants us to pray God will send?
- Are you a worker?

Day Six: Matt. 6:5–8 — Pray in secret

- What different kinds of people are described here?
- Which are you most like, and why?

Day Seven: Luke 18:1–8 — Persistence in prayer

- What is the main point of this story?
- Why did Jesus tell it?
- In what areas do you need to be more persistent in prayer?

If you like, continue this project by having family members find other references to prayer. (You may want to use a concordance or other reference books.) As you learn more about God's instructions for prayer, you may find both your understanding of prayer and your actual prayers changing.

~ • ~

The LORD is far from the wicked but he hears the prayer of the righteous.

PROVERBS 15:29

Reflections of God in a Gallery of Praise

Focus: God's creation

The apostle Paul declared in Romans 1:20, "For since the creation of the world God's invisible qualities—his eternal power and divine nature—have been clearly seen, being understood from what has been made."

Every created thing reflects the Lord's glory and power, so why not use His creation to inspire your family's praise of God? Set up an area in your home such as a bookshelf or the fireplace mantel to place objects that represent God's glory to you and your family. Then encourage family members to fill this area with things that inspire them to praise God. For example, they might fill your chosen spot with items like

- dried flower petals,
- pictures of your family,
- a bird's nest,
- a puppy's collar,
- a card with a favorite Scripture verse written on it,
- a small musical instrument,
- a postcard from the Grand Canyon,

- a child's drawing,
- a pine cone.

Work together to arrange the items into a miniature "art gallery of God's praise," creating small "exhibits" for each one. When your gallery of praise is ready, have your family look through it as they pray together. Include in your prayers moments when family members tell God, "Lord, I see your glory in the things you've created. In this [name something from your gallery], I see Your [name a character quality of God's]."

You may also want to ask Him to help your family be good stewards of the gifts God has given us in creation. We can express our thanks to God for what He's made by caring for the world around us.

~ • ~

I have not stopped giving thanks for you, remembering you in my prayers.

EPHESIANS 1:16

It's on the Map

Focus: Praying for people we don't know

Purchase a map of the world or the country in which you live. Place this map on a bulletin board. Next, give each family member a dart and have him or her throw it at the map. (Older family members may want to help younger children do this safely.) Have family members pray for people who live in the areas that have been "pinpointed" by the darts.

For example, if a dart hits Colorado, everyone can pray for the people of the entire state. The more detailed your map is, the more specific you can be as to which areas you pray for. Be sure to explain a bit about the area you're praying for to younger family members who don't yet have much knowledge of geography.

If you'd like, do a bit of research about the areas on which the darts stick. Go to the local library and use encyclopedias, newspapers, and periodicals to learn more about the countries, states, or cities you've pinpointed. Perhaps there's been war or political unrest or a natural disaster. Or, you may find the area to be enjoying wonderful weather and a low crime rate. Use the information to pray the next time your family gathers, and offer praises more specifically for the people living there.

Variation: If you're uncomfortable using pointed darts with your children, you may want to try damp suction darts. Or young children may enjoy spinning a globe and letting their finger drag along the surface until the globe stops. Then they can pray for the people in the area where their finger is resting.

~ • ~

If my people, who are called by my name, will humble themselves and pray and seek my face and turn from their wicked ways, then will I hear from heaven and will forgive their sin and will heal their land.

2 CHRONICLES 7:14

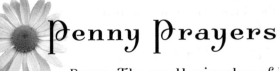

Penny Prayers

Focus: The small miracles of life

Many times we fail to notice what God is doing around us. We might forget to thank Him for an answered prayer or may simply not pay attention to the small miracles of safety, life, and beauty around us. This prayer activity serves as a way to be sure God gets all the "credit."

Place an empty jar where it can be seen easily in your home. Then gather your family and say, "Each time you see God's hand at work in answer to a prayer, put a penny in this jar." (You may want to supply each person with a handful of pennies.) Explain that a penny could be placed in the jar when

- a prayer is answered,
- you see a change in a person or situation you've been praying about,
- you are kept safe in a dangerous situation,
- your attitude is one of joy even in a difficult time or situation.

Have family members think of other examples of God being at work when a penny might be dropped into the jar. Then briefly pray, asking

God to help family members be more aware of His hand throughout the week.

After a week, gather again to see how many coins are in the jar. Count the pennies, then have each person tell about one or two times he or she put one in the jar. Spend a few minutes thanking God for the riches of answered prayer and for reminding your family that He is always at work!

Return the jar to its spot for the upcoming week. After the jar has a good number of pennies in it, allow your children to choose a way to use the coins to purchase a gift for someone. For example, kids might want to buy one or two flowers for a neighbor, or a can of food for a local soup kitchen.

I pray that you may be active in sharing your faith, so that you will have a full understanding of every good thing we have in Christ.

PHILEMON 1:6

Word of the Day

Focus: Thanking God each day

Begin this prayer activity on the last day of a month. Before you start, you'll need a jar, a pen, and twenty-eight to thirty-one slips of paper.

Tell your family, "Let's think of one thing we can thank God for each day of this next month." For example, if the month beginning the next day has thirty days, you'll want to come up with thirty things to thank God for over the next month.

Brainstorm together something to write on each slip of paper. You could include the names of each family member on the slips of paper.

When you have the desired number, fold the paper slips and place them in the jar. On the following morning, ask one family member to reach into the jar and select a slip of paper. Read aloud whatever is written, then tape the paper in a place where everyone will see it (such as on the milk carton or on the bathroom mirror). For the entire day let your prayers include thanking God for what is written on the paper.

The next morning, take down the previous day's item of thanks and have another family member select a new paper. Repeat this each day of the month until all the slips of paper have been used and God has been thanked repeatedly for each one.

But Jesus often withdrew to lonely places and prayed.

LUKE 5:16

Little Reminders

Focus: Reminders to pray for each other

When your family comes together to pray, talk about how hard it can be to remember to pray for each other during the day. Then explain that you've found a fun way of reminding family members to pray for each other. Each day for the next week, you'll all do or wear something in common. Whenever you notice these things, it will serve as a reminder to pray for each other.

Here are some suggestions for reminders, but you can use whatever works for your family.

Day One: Put on each family member's left knee an adhesive bandage (whether it's needed or not!).

Day Two: Draw a smiley face on the back of each person's right hand.

Day Three: Have family members lace their shoes backwards, so that the bow will be near the toes instead of near the ankles. Those who wear Velcro-closing shoes can cross the straps into an X instead of pulling them straight across.

Day Four: Give each person a small pebble to put into his or her pocket.

Day Five: Ask everyone to wear the same color shirt for the day.

Day Six: Pin a safety pin to the left sleeve of each family member's shirt or blouse.

Day Seven: Tie a narrow ribbon or length of yarn around each person's right wrist.

At the end of the week, ask your family members how well the little reminders to pray worked.

~ • ~

The smoke of the incense, together with the prayers of the saints, went up before God from the angel's hand.

REVELATION 8:4

MONTHLY

Prayer Activities

Scripture Prayers

Focus: Prayers from the Bible

Copy each of the following Bible passages on separate 3" x 5" cards:

- I will praise you, O Lord, with all my heart; I will tell of all your wonders. I will be glad and rejoice in you; I will sing praise to your name, O Most High. (Ps. 9:1–2)
- To you, O Lord, I lift up my soul; in you I trust, O my God. Do not let me be put to shame, nor let my enemies triumph over me. No one whose hope is in you will ever be put to shame, but they will be put to shame who are treacherous without excuse. Show me your ways, O Lord, teach me your paths; guide me in your truth and teach me, for you are God my Savior, and my hope is in you all day long. (Ps. 25:1–5)
- Our Father in heaven, hallowed be your name, your kingdom come, your will be done on earth as it is in heaven. Give us today our daily bread. Forgive us our debts, as we also have forgiven our debtors. And lead us not into temptation, but deliver us from the evil one. (Matt. 6:9–13)
- For this reason I kneel before the Father, from whom his whole

family in heaven and on earth derives its name. I pray that out of his glorious riches he may strengthen you with power through his Spirit in your inner being, so that Christ may dwell in your hearts through faith. (Eph. 3:14–17)

- And I pray that you, being rooted and established in love, may have power, together with all the saints, to grasp how wide and long and high and deep is the love of Christ, and to know this love that surpasses knowledge—that you may be filled to the measure of all the fullness of God. (Eph. 3:17–19)
- There is no one holy like the LORD; there is no one besides you; there is no Rock like our God. (1 Sam. 2:2)
- How great you are, O Sovereign LORD! There is no one like you, and there is no God but you, as we have heard with our own ears. (2 Sam. 7:22)
- LORD, I have heard of your fame; I stand in awe of your deeds, O LORD. Renew them in our day, in our time make them known. (Hab. 3:2)
- As the deer pants for streams of water, so my soul pants for you, O God. My soul thirsts for God, for the living God. (Ps. 42:1–2)
- But let justice roll on like a river, righteousness like a never-failing stream! (Amos 5:24)
- Create in me a pure heart, O God, and renew a steadfast spirit within me. Restore to me the joy of your salvation and grant me a willing spirit, to sustain me. (Ps. 51:10,12)
- Hear my cry, O God; listen to my prayer. From the ends of the earth I call to you, I call as my heart grows faint; lead me to the rock that is higher than I. For you have been my refuge, a strong tower against the foe. (Ps. 61:1–3)
- Teach me your way, O LORD, and I will walk in your truth; give me an undivided heart, that I may fear your name. (Ps. 86:11)
- I will exalt you, my God the King; I will praise your name for

ever and ever. Every day I will praise you and extol your name for ever and ever. (Ps. 145:1–2)

Place the cards in a stack on a table. Before your evening meal, have each family member who knows how to read take a card from the top of the stack. Then take turns reading aloud these prayers from the Bible. If the words or phrases are too difficult for young children to understand, explain what they mean.

When your turn is over, return the card to the bottom of the stack to be used at another meal. Let these verses be your mealtime prayer.

As you and other family members discover other prayers in the Bible that are meaningful to your lives, write them on cards and add them to the stack. The book of Psalms is full of prayers with a wide variety of meanings (praising God, thanking God, asking for help). It's a great place to have family members look for more verses if you'd like to add more.

In the same way, the Spirit helps us in our weakness. We do not know what we ought to pray for, but the Spirit himself intercedes for us with groans that words cannot express.

ROMANS 8:26

Puzzling Answers

Focus: Recognizing answered prayers

For this prayer activity, you'll need a jigsaw puzzle. Choose the size and difficulty of your puzzle according to the ages and abilities of your family. If your kids are preschoolers, a 30- to 40-piece puzzle will work best. For school-age children and older, choose a puzzle with 50 to 150 pieces. (You probably won't want a puzzle with more than 150 pieces.)

Place the puzzle pieces and a pen on a card table or another flat surface where they can be left for a period. Then explain to your family that this puzzle will be put together as prayers are answered in your home. Here's how it works.

Every time a person in your family realizes that God has answered a prayer, he or she should choose a puzzle piece. On the back of the piece, the person writes a word or two (depending on the size of the piece) as a reminder of what the answer to prayer was.

For example, "A+" might be an answer to a prayer for help on a spelling test. "Sweet dreams" might mean a child's prayers not to have nightmares was answered. Or, "$" could remind a college student (or the student's parents) that God provided money to make the tuition payment.

When two puzzle pieces have been written on, they can be attached together. Leave the puzzle pieces out until each piece has something written on the back and has been attached to the rest of the puzzle.

When the puzzle is complete, have your family admire the finished product. Then thank God for being involved in your family's prayers. Thank Him for using your prayers to demonstrate the greater picture of His power.

If you like, leave the puzzle on display for a while as a reminder of all the prayers God has answered. Then take the puzzle apart and store it for later use. When you do pull it out again, see if family members can remember what the answers to prayer were by the notes written on each puzzle piece.

~ • ~

Therefore confess your sins to each other and pray for each other so that you may be healed. The prayer of a righteous man is powerful and effective.

JAMES 5:16

Pray for Me When This You See

Focus: Remembering needs of family members

The next time your family is together, ask each person to think of an item that could regularly be used to represent him or her. It should be something that can be used again and again, and that other family members would associate with its owner. For example, a younger family member might have a special teddy bear that could represent him or her. A sports fan might use a team hat or pennant. A book lover might use a library card, a chocoholic might use an empty candy wrapper, or the family musician might choose a favorite CD or cassette case.

When each person has chosen an item, have everyone show what his or her item is and, if necessary, explain why it was chosen. Then determine together a spot that everyone sees daily, such as a coffee or end table, mantel, or kitchen counter. Name this space the "Prayer Spot."

Then tell your family, "For the next month, whenever you feel like you need us to pray for you, put your item on the Prayer Spot to remind the rest of us that you need prayer." For example, if LaKeisha is headed to the doctor for an annual shot, she might put her stuffed camel on the Prayer Spot. If Mom is making a special presentation at work, she might put her coffee mug on the Prayer Spot.

As the days of the month progress, be sure to pray for those who put their representative items on the Prayer Spot. If you like, leave a small note pad at the Prayer Spot so people can specify why they need prayer. Or, ask family members to explain their need for prayer during a meal or at another time you regularly gather. This will help others to pray more specifically.

⌒ • ⌒

But I cry to you for help, O LORD; in the morning my prayer comes before you.

PSALM 88:13

Prayer Calendar

Focus: A month of guided prayer

For each day of the next month, refer to the appropriate date, and pray as directed. If you like, copy the directions onto a large, blank wall calendar to help your family remember to pray each day.

Family members may wish to refer to the prayer calendar on their own, or you might share the topic of prayer at a specified time, such as breakfast or dinner, and pray together each day for the month.

1. Thank God for each person living in your house.
2. Pray for your teacher, supervisor, or another person of authority.
3. Pray for an elderly person you know that lives alone.
4. Thank God for a special friend.
5. Ask God's forgiveness for things you have done wrong.
6. Sing a song (alone or as a family) that tells God how great He is.
7. Pray for the president of our country.
8. Thank God for an extended family member (grandparent, cousin, etc.)

9. Read Psalm 66:1–4 together, then shout to God, "How awesome are Your deeds!"
10. Thank God for a person who makes your life difficult.
11. Pray for your neighbors.
12. Thank God for the comforts of your life such as food, a home, and clothing.
13. Ask God to show each person in your family His love in a special way today.
14. Tell God you're sorry for not always obeying Him, and thank Him for loving you still.
15. Pray for someone you've read about in the newspaper or heard about on the news.
16. Thank God for His creation and tell Him one way you'll take care of it.
17. Pray for the leaders of your church such as Sunday school teachers, pastors, and youth leaders.
18. Tell God how much you appreciate His love.
19. Thank God for giving us the Bible.
20. Pray for the missionaries that you or your church supports. Also pray for the people they are reaching in their ministry.
21. Ask God to help you show love to each person you talk to today.
22. Pray for people who are living in an area torn by war. Ask God to restore peace to that land.
23. Pray for someone who is sick or sad.
24. Praise God for sending His Holy Spirit.
25. Pray for your coworkers, schoolmates, or others you come into contact with daily.
26. Thank God for your parents.
27. Ask God to help you grow closer to Him.
28. Pray for the staff at your church, such as secretaries, custodians, and so on.

29. Tell God how much you appreciate His forgiveness.
30. Ask God to help you show kindness to others today.
31. Thank God for the wonderful gift of Jesus.

~ • ~

I will praise the LORD, who counsels me; even at night my heart instructs me.

PSALM 16:7

Prayer Notebook

Focus: Long-term prayer needs

For this activity you'll need a picture of each family member. Give each person his or her picture along with a blank sheet of notebook paper and a pen or pencil. Have family members tape or glue their pictures at the top of the paper.

Have everyone write two or three ongoing prayer requests they have that will need prayer for the next three to six months. For example,

- A parent may have an ongoing request for patience.
- A child may want prayer for understanding a difficult school subject.
- Someone may need of healing of a long-term illness or condition.

Help younger family members write their requests. When the papers are completed, place them in a notebook. Then set the notebook on a coffee table or another convenient location. Each day, turn the page to a different family member's page. You can pray together as a family for the pictured person, or leave the book out for those who pass by to see as a reminder to pray.

Update the pages every six months or so. If you like, tell extended family members (aunts, uncles, grandparents, cousins) what you're doing, and have them send pictures and request pages to be added to your book as well.

⌒ • ⌒

In the same way, let your light shine before men, that they may see your good deeds and praise your Father in heaven.

MATTHEW 5:16

Book of Answered Prayers

Focus: Recording prayers and praises

This project is for your family to work on over a long period. You'll need either a notebook or a blank book such as a journal.

Begin by asking everyone to think of one or two prayers God has answered. It can be a recent answer to prayer or one that happened years ago. Then have family members tell about these answered prayers. After each person shares, write the details of the prayer and how it was answered in the book. Family members may want to write in the information themselves, or one family member can be given the role of "scribe." Begin a new entry for each answered prayer.

When each person has made at least one entry in the book, begin interviewing other people about their answers to prayer:

- Ask guests who visit your home to share a time God answered their prayers.
- Ask leaders from your church such as pastors, Sunday school teachers, or volunteer staff to share answered prayers.

- Talk with extended family members (grandparents, aunts, uncles, cousins, stepbrothers or stepsisters) and include their answers.
- Ask other friends or acquaintances, as you like!

As time goes by, your entries will begin to fill page after page with answers to prayer. Occasionally read through some of the entries as a family to remind yourselves how God has worked in the lives of many people over the course of many, many years!

~ • ~

Amen! Praise and glory and wisdom and thanks and honor and power and strength be to our God for ever and ever. Amen!

REVELATION 7:12

Far from Home

Focus: Remembering others in prayer

Use this prayer adventure when a family member will be away from home for several days. It could be used when a parent is on a business trip, when a child spends a week at camp, during those first nervous days of school, or any other time when family members will be separated for a length of time.

Come together as a family, and remind everyone of the upcoming separation. Then read the following passages together.

> *I thank God, whom I serve, as my forefathers did, with a clear conscience, as night and day I constantly remember you in my prayers.*
>
> 2 TIMOTHY 1:3

> *In all my prayers for all of you, I always pray with joy because of your partnership in the gospel from the first day until now.*
>
> PHILIPPIANS 1:4–5

> *I have not stopped giving thanks for you, remembering you in my prayers.*
>
> EPHESIANS 1:16

Then ask your family these questions:

- Why do you think it's important to pray for each other when we're apart?
- How do you feel when you know someone far away is praying for you?
- As our family experiences time apart, what should we remember to pray about? (For example, safety, freedom from fear, or whatever the needs are in your specific situation.)

Together, determine one or more specific times during the day for everyone to remember to pray. Choose a time when family members can be reminded to pray. For example, your family might choose to pray at 10:30 a.m. One child will be reminded to pray because a school bell rings at this time. Mom can set the alarm on her computer at work, Dad has an alarm on his digital watch, and another child will be reminded by the chiming of the clock at home. Then have everyone commit to pray for the needs you've discussed when the bells start ringing the next day.

If your time of separation is only one day, you may want to be reminded to pray several times through the day. If the time apart will be lengthy, have only one or two prayer reminders each day.

When the family is reunited, talk about how everyone felt knowing that others were praying at the same time during the day. How did you see your specific prayers answered?

Now my God, may your eyes be open and your ears attentive to the prayers offered in this place.

2 CHRONICLES 6:40

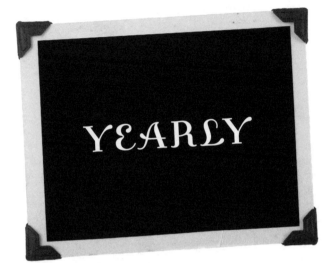

YEARLY

Prayer Activities

Sponsored in Prayer

Focus: Caring for a child through prayer

You've probably seen or read appeals to sponsor a child financially through a relief organization. Perhaps your family even has "adopted" a child in another country through one of these charities. In this activity, your family will sponsor a child through prayer.

First, choose a child your family would like to pray for. If you already sponsor a child financially, you could choose that child, but you could choose a child you've read about in the newspaper, a child at school, a missing child, or any other young person your family feels is in need of regular prayer.

If possible, obtain a picture of your chosen child, and keep it on your refrigerator or another prominent location. If a picture isn't available, select another object that will represent this person to your family. You might choose a small flag from the country where the child lives. Or, if your chosen child is in need of medical attention, you might use a get-well card as your reminder.

Over the next year, pray regularly for this child making your prayers as specific as possible. If it's appropriate, your family may also want to send notes of encouragement or make other similar gestures to show your love and concern for this child.

After a year, thank God for any changes you've seen in this child. Then let your family decide if they'd like to continue praying for this child, or if they'd like to choose another to pray for during the coming year.

~ • ~

Be joyful in hope, patient in affliction, faithful in prayer.

ROMANS 12:12

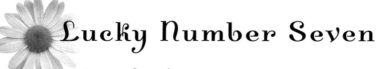

Lucky Number Seven

Focus: Enemies

When you've gathered to pray together, read the following verse.

> *Then Peter came to Jesus and asked, "Lord, how many times shall I forgive my brother when he sins against me? Up to seven times?" Jesus answered, "I tell you, not seven times, but seventy-seven times."*

MATTHEW 18:21–22

Discuss what this verse means. Ask your family, "Have you ever forgiven one person that many times? Has someone had to forgive you that many times?"

Then read this verse aloud:

> *But I tell you: Love your enemies and pray for those who persecute you.*

MATTHEW 5:44

Talk about how Jesus not only wants us to forgive people who make our lives difficult, but He also wants us to love them and pray for them!

Next, have each family member tell about one person that makes life hard. This could be a bully at school, a "friend" who gossips behind your back, a boss or coworker that makes work unpleasant, a neighbor who plays music too loud, or a teacher who seems to take pleasure in ridiculing you. Then ask family members how they feel about following God's instructions and praying for these "enemies."

Suggest that your family use the number seven as a reminder to pray for the people who annoy us. On every day of the month that has a seven in it, join together in prayer for your enemies. Also take time during these prayer gatherings to share any ways you're finding these prayers answered. How is God changing your attitude toward this person or the situation? How is God helping you to love your enemies?

As time (and days with sevens in them) goes by, you may find yourself and other family members taking some of these "enemies" off of that list, and adding them to your list of friends!

⁓ • ⁓

I always thank my God as I remember you in my prayers, because I hear about your faith in the Lord Jesus and your love for all the saints.

PHILEMON 1:4–5

special occasion

Prayer Activities

Letters to God

Focus: Advent or New Year's

The beginning of a new year is a good time to evaluate where you've been and what your goals are for the coming year. This activity could be used at any time, but we suggest using it to kick off a new calendar year. It could also be used at the beginning of Advent, the start of a new church year.

As you come together to pray, explain that we can communicate to God by writing our thoughts to Him. Give each person a piece of paper and pen or pencil. Then say, "Let's begin the new year by writing letters of prayer to God!"

Ask family members to write down areas where they need help from God, things they'd like to thank God for, and so on. Children who don't know how to write yet may draw a picture expressing their thoughts to God or have an older family member help them.

When each person has completed his or her letter, give everyone the opportunity to read the letters aloud in prayer. If anyone is uncomfortable with this, have everyone read his or her letters silently in prayer.

Then have each one seal his or her letter in an envelope, writing his or her name and the date on the outside. Put the envelopes in a place for safekeeping. Make a notation on your calendar that in one year you will give the letters to each family member. (If you're a bit forgetful, you also might want to note where you've stored the letters!)

When the year has passed, distribute each prayer letter to its owner. Let family members read their prayers from a year ago. Take time to share how prayers have been answered, how situations have changed, and how God is still working in the areas mentioned in each letter. Thank God for what He's done, and pray for continued support with ongoing concerns.

⌒ • ⌒

> *Then Hannah prayed and said: "My heart rejoices in the LORD; in the LORD my horn is lifted high. My mouth boasts over my enemies, for I delight in your deliverance."*

I SAMUEL 2:1

Christmas-Card Prayers

Focus: Remembering friends after Christmas

This Christmas when you're taking down the decorations, set aside all the cards and newsletters your family received. Place them in a basket, a napkin holder, or even a shoebox. Set the container on or near your dining-room table.

Each evening during dinner, take the top card from the stack and read it aloud. As a family, talk about the person or family. You could also take time to let family members relate special memories they have of this person or family.

When you're ready, pray for the individual or family that sent the card or newsletter. Mention specific praises or needs, then return the card to the bottom of the stack.

In your own Christmas cards and letters, let people know your family will be remembering and praying for others during the next year. It might just increase the number of cards you receive!

By day the Lord *directs his love, at night his song is with me—a prayer to the God of my life.*

PSALM 42:8

Out of the Darkness

Focus: Good Friday or Easter

Have your family squeeze together into the smallest, darkest space of your home. If you can fit, a closet is the best. Or, if you have a large family, a dark bathroom will work.

When you're all together, tell your family about Jesus' death on the cross and how He was buried in a dark tomb. (If you need a refresher on the details of this story, read the account given in Mark 15:21–47.)

Explain that just as the tomb was without light, our hearts are without light. Ask family members to think of things that make our hearts dark. Then pray together that God would remove these things from your lives.

Remind your family that Jesus arose from the dead! (Find the details in Mark 16.) Let the youngest family member open the door and release you all from the dark. After you've untangled yourselves from the cramped darkness, talk about how Jesus rose from the dead and brought light into our lives. Then spend a few minutes thanking God for sending Jesus, for bringing Him back to life, and for giving us life because of His love!

⌒ • ⌒

He prays to God and finds favor with him, he sees God's face and shouts for joy; he is restored by God to his righteous state.

JOB 33:26

Star-Spangled Prayer

Focus: Independence Day

This activity can be used throughout the year, but we find it goes well with July 4. You'll need an American flag, but if you can't find the real thing, a picture of one will work, too.

As your family comes together for prayer, ask if anyone knows what the stars and stripes on the flag represent. If not, explain that each star represents one of the fifty states in the Union, and each stripe represents one of the original thirteen colonies. The colors of the flag also have meaning. Red symbolizes courage, white is for purity, and blue represents justice.

As you examine and discuss the flag, explain to your family that you'd like to use the flag and its symbolism as a guide to prayer.

- For every star on the flag, think of something your family is thankful for. Have different family members offer a one-sentence prayer of thanksgiving. For example, "Thank You, Lord, that we are free to worship You in our country," or "Thanks, God, for giving us food each day." Continue until you've thanked God fifty times. (You may want to use this part of the activity over the course of several days or a week.)

- As the blue field behind the stars represents justice, pray for people who are oppressed and in need of justice. You may want to include people in other countries who don't enjoy the freedoms we do in America. You could also pray for Christians in other countries who can't express their faith.
- For each of the six white stripes, ask God to bring purity to a different area of your lives, including your speech toward each other, your actions, and so on.
- Pray for courage as guided by the flag's seven red stripes. A family member may need bravery to stand up for his or her beliefs at school or work, or you may all need courage to share about God's love to an unfriendly neighbor.

Close your time together by praying for America, asking God to bring guidance and to show His love to all who live under this flag.

Variation: If you live in a country other than the United States of America, use your flag and a national holiday to create a prayer adventure similar to this one. Research the symbols and colors of your national flag and determine ways to use these as a guide for prayer. Consider the specific needs of your country as well as reasons you are thankful for your country.

The LORD has heard my cry for mercy; the LORD accepts my prayer.

PSALM 6:9

Travel Time with God

Focus: Summer Vacation

Use this prayer activity the next time your family hits the road on a trip.

- Every time you see cattle, thank God for a different person in the car, and tell one reason you're glad this person is along on the journey.
- When you see a sign for a rest stop, sing a hymn or chorus of a praise song. (In some cases, the "Hallelujah" chorus may be appropriate.)
- Each time you pass a mile marker ending in 00, pray for the driver of your car. Ask God to keep this person alert and to give guidance as he or she drives the car.
- Be on the lookout for a particular favorite fast-food restaurant chain. When that restaurant is spotted, thank God for the friends or family you'll be seeing on this trip.

You can add to these suggestions to fit the needs and interests of your family. For example, every time you see a license plate from a specific state, pray for a specific request. Or each time you see a sign with blue on it, thank God for good weather. Use this prayer activity as often as you'd like during your trip, letting family members change the items to look for and the prayers to go with them.

~ • ~

Pray that the LORD your God will tell us where we should go and what we should do.

JEREMIAH 42:3

Birthday Candle Prayers

Focus: Birthdays

Start this new tradition on the next birthday of a family member. When you're ready to have the birthday boy or girl blow out the candles, ask each person to think silently of something they're thankful for about the person celebrating today. Then, as you light each candle, have people take turns praying out loud a short, one-sentence prayer of thanks about the birthday person.

For example, if Dillon is turning six, family members might say,

- "God, thanks that Dillon has lots of energy."
- "Thank You for Dillon's happy smile."
- "Lord, I'm glad for Dillon's helpful attitude."
- "I'm thankful that Dillon gives great hugs."
- "God, thank You for helping Dillon learn to tie his own shoes."
- "Thanks for sending Dillon to our family!"

When a prayer for each candle has been offered, sing "Happy Birthday" and have the child blow out the candles.

This tradition can be carried on for every family member, no matter how old or young. However, once you get into the teen years and above you may find it safer to pray *before* lighting the candles—unless you're fast pray-ers or have tall candles!

Option: This prayer adventure may also be used to celebrate baptism anniversaries. Light a baptismal candle to remember and rejoice at new birth.

⌁ • ⌁

I pray that out of his glorious riches he may strengthen you with power through his Spirit in your inner being.

EPHESIANS 3:16

Scripture Index

Mike & Amy Nappa

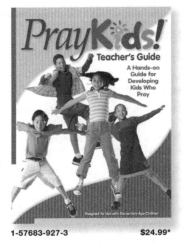

*Pray*Kids!®

Encourage a Lifetime of Passion for Christ through Prayer

Get elementary-age children excited about prayer! *Pray*Kids! is a kid-friendly publication that opens up the world of prayer with Bible-based stories, global prayer guides, hands-on activities, games, and more! Designed to be used any time of year, in any setting.

Issues Available:

(All come in packs of 10 for $6.99*)

Praise
Issue 1 (#1600062067)

Confession
Issue 2 (Item #26)

Thankfulness
Issue 3 (#1600060420)

Intercession
Issue 4 (#1600060439)

Spiritual Warfare
Issue 5 (#1600060447)

Hearing God
Issue 6 (#1600060455)

Forgiveness
Issue 7 (Item #31)

Prayerwalking
Issue 8 (Item #32)

Fasting
Issue 9 (Item #33)

Time with Jesus
Issue 10 (Item #34)

Agreement
Issue 11 (Item #35)

Why Prayer Works
Issue 12 (Item #36)

Seeking God
Issue 13 (Item #37)

Petition
Issue 14 (Item #38)

Jesus' Prayer Life
Issue 15 (Item #39)

Authority/ Submission
Issue 16 (Item #40)

The Holy Spirit
Issue 17 (Item #41)

Surrender
Issue 18 (Item #42)

Prayer Styles
Issue 19 (Item #43)

Faith
Issue 20 (Item #44)

Praying for the Lost
Issue 21 (Item #45)

God's Character
Issue 22 (Item #46)

Boldness
Issue 23 (Item #47)

Perseverance
Issue 24 (Item #48)

Contemplative Prayer
Issue 25 (Item #49)

Praying God's Will
Issue 26 (Item #50)

Four sampler packs are also available for $8.00* per pack! Each pack includes one copy of each listed issue. Choose from:

Issues 1-6 (#1600060862)
Issues 7-12 (#1600060870)

Issues 13-19 (#1600060889)
Issues 20-26 (#1600060897)

Inspire your kids to pray!

Order today! Call 1-800-366-7788 (or 1-719-548-9222) 7am-5pm M-F, MST
Save 20% by ordering online at www.praykids.com
*plus shipping/handling and applicable sales tax